How To Buy
A Used Car...
Successfully

D0006518

How To Buy A Used Car... Successfully

✔ lemon vs. cream puff
✔ shopping
✔ negotiating
✔ pricing vs. value

Bill Bacon 1937-

Auto Merit
Germantown, Tennessee

Additional copies of this book may be ordered through bookstores or by sending $8.95 plus $2.75 for postage and handling to
Publishers Distribution Service
121 E. Front Street, Suite 203
Traverse City, MI 49684
1-800-345-0096

Illustrations by James Bacon

Publisher's Cataloging-in-Publication Data

Bacon, Bill, 1937 -
    Buying a used car—successfully / by Bill Bacon—
Germantown, Tennessee : Auto Merit.
      p.   ill.   cm.
    Includes bibliography and index.
    ISBN: 0-9632723-0-6
    1. Used cars—Purchasing. 2. Automobiles—Purchasing.
I. Title.
TL 162.B33   1992
629.222—dc20   92-71087

Manufactured in the United States of America.

10 9 8 7 6 5 4 3 2 1

Book Design by Alex Moore / PDS

This book is dedicated to my Dad. He bought many used cars and they never turned out to be what he hoped they were. But his high hopes, spirit of adventure, and willingness to try again started my education on how to buy a used car. I could never have written this book without those early experiences.

Acknowledgments

There are many people to thank for their help in preparing this manuscript, and I hesitate to do so because I am bound to leave someone out. Without my wife Verna's support and encouragement, I would never have gotten it done. My two sons, Paul and Ken (who are also used-car buyers who learned from their Dad's mistakes), gave valuable input from their own experiences. My brother's son, James Bacon, did a magnificent job of turning rough ideas into helpful illustrations. My friend Lee Whipple did an incredibly detailed critique of the manuscript instead of enjoying his vacation in Hot Springs. Other friends also helped—Tom Hall, George Word, Jack Harja, Chris King, Brad Champlin, Terry Felts. And my Mom helped a lot, because she knew all the time that I could do it.

Preface

Buying a used car is the best way to get a real bargain in automobiles. There are some great choices today! But you face a tougher challenge than ever before in making the right choice. Cars today cost more and are more complicated. There are more makes and models to choose from. This book will help you answer the questions: Is this the car I would *really* like to own? Will it be reliable? How should I go about bargaining? What about financing, insurance, and titles? Getting the right answers will make you a happy used-car buyer!

Contents

Introduction

Most of us have bought a used car at least once. Most of us will buy another one. Over three-fourths of the cars sold are previously-owned cars.

Used cars are certainly a great bargain. After only four years, a car that sold for $18,000 when new may cost only $6,000 today - and still be in great shape. But how do you get a bargain without a surprise? There are many previously-owned cars out there that are going to be a lot of trouble and expense for their next owner. How can you tell a bargain from a problem? What is a fair price?

A Car That Sold For $18,000 When New
May Only Cost $6,000 Today

This book was written to help you make a better choice. Each chapter will take you through a step in the process of:

- What do I really want?
- Where can I find It?
- What is it worth?
- How can I negotiate a good price?
- What problems does it have?
- How can I finance it?
- Can I get a breakdown warranty?
- What about insurance?
- What about titles, taxes, and tags?
- How do I take care of my car when I get it home?

When you are finished, you will be able to look after your own interests better, have more confidence, and *enjoy* your car hunting. It's YOUR money. And usually a lot of it. A car is a major financial decision for most of us. You ought to be able to make your money work for you - and have fun, too. A good car is a real joy to own. Happy hunting!

Before you go car shopping, please read or at least skim through each chapter in this book. Some sections you may use more than others. But be aware of the contents of each chapter, especially Chapter 4, "Checking it out," so that you can do a good job of making your money work for you and avoid the major surprises that may be waiting out there for you.

Please understand my use of the male pronoun in the text. Of course, women as well as men buy and sell used cars. This book is written as much for women as men.

But I found that constant use of "he/she" or "they" was clumsy and sometimes confusing. Until there is a better solution, please accept "he" as meaning either gender.

How To Buy
A Used Car...
Successfully

First, Get A Notebook

Getting Started

Keeping Notes

Before you do anything else, get yourself a spiral or loose-leaf notebook to write down the various pieces of information you will be gathering in order to make good decisions. There are several decisions to make and a lot of choices. It will help you to write it down as you go.

You might begin by organizing your book with a few pages each for:

- What you are looking for
- Cars you have looked at
- Dealers/Sources
- Insurance

Or, you might want to make a page for each car you investigate, in which case each page might have a place to write down:

- Make, Model, and Year
- Accessories and Optional Equipment
- Seller
- Price
- Reliability/Service
- Condition
- Problems
- Mileage

- Insurance Cost
- Economy of Operation
- Appearance
- Performance
- Comfort
- Safety
- Resale Value
- Overall Suitability (do I LIKE it?)

Add or delete items from the above lists based on your own values and priorities. Write down what will be important to you when trying to make your final decisions. There is a handy list of "WHAT I WANT - features and accessories" in the Appendix that might help you decide what you want.

If that seems unduly complicated, just date each page and keep notes chronologically as a log book. Even this simple step will add immeasurably to your recall of facts. After a little looking, the various cars and prices will begin to run together in your mind. You will be very glad you wrote down the details.

An important advantage of writing all this down is that you will be car shopping for the rest of your life! The car you buy this time will need to be replaced some day, and you will go through this process all over again. If you have written down what you have done at each step, you will have a head start next time. It's a certainty that you will get better at it as you shop, and with each car you buy you will become a more experienced and expert buyer in getting what you want. So keep your notebook handy so as to take best advantage of what you learn each time.

Knowing What You Want

Cars are an important part of our American lifestyle. Most of us spend as much or more on our cars as we do on our housing. Over your lifetime you may actually spend more on your cars than housing, because you will be constantly replacing your cars - a never-ending process! It is very important for you to be aware of your own particular motivation for spending this much money so that you can best meet your own wants and needs.

There are many different reasons for buying a car. And there are dozens of "experts" who will try to tell you which car is best. But don't forget that *you* are the real expert in the matter of what you really want. Sit down and think through the primary purpose for the car. Is it for business, pleasure, around-town, long trips, commuting, or for your children to drive to school? Just how important are appearance, reliability, comfort, safety, performance, price, operating cost, and resale value? Some of these can be conflicting choices.

Is reliability more important than appearance? Is performance more important than comfort or reliability? Is low purchase price more important than resale value?

Make a list of how important each item is to you. The list in the Appendix has most of the items you might want to consider. Remember, some of these are mutually exclusive. If price is most important, you can't insist on all the options and high resale value. You get what you pay for. If you are careful, you can pay for only what you want and make your money go a lot further in satisfying your own personal preferences.

But don't make it *too* scientific! The list is only there to help you think through what you want the most. The best measure of the car is, after all, "Is this the car I *really* want to spend *my* money on compared to all the others?"

Start with the list "WHAT I WANT" from the Appendix and make up your wish list. Then make copies of the "AUTOMOBILE RATING" sheet from the Appendix. You will use these to rate each individual car you consider purchasing. This will help you determine which of your many choices will suit you best. The "WHAT I WANT" list will help you summarize what is most important to you about any potential car. The "RATING" sheet lets you compare those wants to each specific car you consider.

Don't be afraid, when you are all finished evaluating, to go with your instincts rather than blindly following your list. The "Right Car" will never be a strictly analytical decision for most of us. Passion can be as important as ration!

Collecting Information

There are two especially important pieces of information you will want to get before you actually get into looking for a specific car: Price and Reliability. You can get excellent information on both.

PRICE

There are several ways to get a good idea of car prices. The simplest, of course, is to just look in the newspaper at the classified section on cars. The local *Auto Exchange/Auto Trader/Wheels & Deals* magazines available in the convenience stores and news stands are also a good source of information on available cars and prices.

There Are Lots Of Good Sources Of Information

You will probably notice a big variation in prices on almost identical cars. How come? First, these are the ASKING prices - what someone *hopes* to sell it for, not necessarily what it *will* sell for. Most everyone advertising a car expects to have to bargain over the final selling price, so most of the prices you see will have a little "cushion" in them for bargaining. So the prices you see are not the real selling prices of those cars. The actual final selling prices will be a bit lower - often $1000 or more lower - because of the bargaining that takes place in buying and selling of cars. If you are using those advertised prices to estimate the actual cash value of a trade-in or a car you

are selling, recognize that you will have to adjust down-
ward a bit to allow for this factor.

Any car is only worth what someone will pay for it. And
some sellers are more desperate than others to sell the
car. But the car itself is obviously a major variable. What
kind of condition is it in? Does it have all the desirable
options? How will I know what is a fair price for any given
car?

PRICING GUIDES

There are industry guidelines for used-car pricing. The
most recognized guide is the *N.A.D.A. Appraisal Guide,*
used by most dealers and banks. Their data is based on
sales reports from car dealers across the country and
adjusted for regional variations. Another good source is
the National Auto Research *Black Book* which is based on
sales results of dealer-only auto auctions across the
country. Some consider the *Black Book* more accurate data
than the *N.A.D.A.* since it is actual sales of actual cars at
wholesale auctions. The *N.A.D.A.* is based on unaudited
"reported" selling prices from dealers. The prices in the
two guides are usually pretty close to each other, so both
are decent guides to use to arrive at a fair market price of
a car. And there are other guides available, too, depending
on the locality and regional habits.

But these guides are only available by subscription. So
what can you, the consumer, use? Your banker or credit
union loan officer can look up particular cars for you in their
N.A.D.A. or Black Book guides. But you may find this to
be inconvenient and time-consuming.

The easiest approach is to get one of the very useful
car pricing guides on the news stands. The most popular

is *Edmunds Used Car Pricing Guide.* This will be well worth its modest price in determining fair prices for the cars you will be considering.

We'll cover pricing again in more detail in Chapter 3.

RELIABILITY

The single biggest concern of most of us buying a used car is: "Am I buying someone else's troubles?" Haven't we all gotten rid of a car because we were concerned about problems, unreliability, or repairs? Many of the cars you will look at are just that kind of a problem waiting to happen to *you!* How will you avoid them? If you choose wisely, your car *will* last longer than the payments.

If You Choose Wisely, Your Car Will
Last Longer Than The Payments

It is possible to buy a used car, save a lot of money compared to buying a new one and still get reliable transportation. Part of the trick is checking out the car thoroughly. We'll do that in Chapter 4. But first you must start with a car that *can* be reliable. There is no substitute for "good breeding", in dogs, horses, and cars!

Some cars can take a lot of abuse and just keep going. Others never seem to be completely fixed. The design and manufacture of each specific make and model has a lot to do with what kind of service you will get from it for years to come. Even the best manufacturers occasionally goof and make a model they are not proud of. You don't want one of these in your driveway even if you have a live-in mechanic.

How do you avoid them? Start by learning from the experiences others have had. Cars with bad reputations generally deserve them. Same is true for good reputations. Allowing a little "windage" for owner loyalty, people that rave about their cars have generally gotten good service from them. So listen to your friends and acquaintances. If you buy a similar make/model, you will be likely to have the same experience.

An even better way to look at the experience of others is to read the *Consumer Reports Annual Auto Issue,* usually the April issue. Subscribe - it's a good publication. Go buy the April issue when it hits the newsstands. Or, if you begin your search during the other 11 months of the year, go to your local library and read it there.

What *Consumer Reports* compiles is the frequency-of-repair and repair cost records of their subscriber's cars - most domestic and foreign cars - manufactured over the last six years. Repairs are by category: air conditioning, paint, brakes, engine, transmission, etc. You can look at the relative reliability experience of over 800,000 cars for just the price of a magazine - an astounding bargain! Although some experts complain that the data is not qualified and sorted by driving habits, mileage, or area of the country, these complaints are trivial compared to the power of this massive data base. There are exceptions, of course, but beware! You might win the lottery, too, but you probably won't. You will be much wiser to expect the average.

One cautionary note may be in order here. Most of the Detroit cars have not really gotten worse over the last ten years, as these repair records might lead you to believe. What has happened is that some of the imports, especially the Japanese, have simply gotten dramatically more reliable. And the ratings are *comparative.*

Domestic Cars Have Not Gotten Worse,
Imports Have Just Gotten Better

So GM, Ford, and Chrysler are struggling to catch up - and for some models they have.

The entire industry has been driven by Federal laws and by market expectations to lower pollution, better fuel mileage, and higher reliability. The good news is that they have made dramatic progress. The bad news is that new car prices have doubled in the same period of time! But that's a powerful reason to go *used*-car hunting - we're going to save even more. So let's get started.

Identifying Candidate Cars

With over 600 makes and models each year to choose from, how are you going to pick one or more to begin with? Well, you probably already have one or more in mind and have seen some interesting candidates in the literature you have assembled. You have a friend that drives a car you think you would like. This is a good place to start.

Over 600 Makes & Models To Choose From Each Year

Just write down a few cars that you think you might like to own. Then look them up in your pricing and reliability guides and compare what you see. Next, go to your newspaper or *Auto Exchange* and look for these or something close - a year earlier or later, a different model, or a "sister" from another make (a Mercury instead of a Ford, for instance).

If you find several possible choices in your price range, you can begin looking now. If not, you need to adjust your criteria until you have a few more to choose from. There are obviously several cars out there somewhere that would suit you just fine. All you have to do is to find them!

Be sure to stretch your mind a little bit when you are making your list of cars to consider. Without stretching

Stretch Your Mind A Little Bit

your budget, you ought to consider a car that is simpler or fancier than you first considered. Maybe a different model or one with different equipment. This will give you better perspective on the one you think you *really* want. You should also consider more than one brand name, at least one foreign make and one domestic make so that you can compare car values in the same price range against your own selection criteria.

While speaking of foreign vs. domestic cars, you will notice in your pricing guide that the foreign used cars, especially the major Japanese brands, are priced higher than the domestic manufacturers (see the pricing chart in the next chapter). The American public has found these to be very desirable used cars and therefore will pay more money to get one. When you look at the frequency-of-repair records in *Consumer Reports,* one of the reasons is obvious. They are designed and built for excellent reliability and economy of operation. And they are responsive and fun to drive. Many of them won "Car of the Year" awards during the Eighties from various American car magazines. Many are very competent cars indeed. Although they are priced higher as used cars, they therefore retain their value better once you own them.

However, there also are good domestic models. You will find that many are a better buy than the most-wanted Japanese makes. Although some don't rank as high in reliability, they will give you very good service at a lower cost. As we have already said, domestic cars did not really get a lot worse. The imports just got dramatically better by comparison. And some domestic models have now just about caught up. So look at the ratings, avoid the obvious "dogs", and compare the values. The best choice is not necessarily the absolute highest rating.

Look at the example price comparisons in the next chapter for 1991 prices of 1988-model-year cars. Now make your own chart for the cars in which you might be interested. Go through your pricing guide and pick out some cars that you might not have considered that are in the same price range as the cars you started with. This might give you some useful alternatives.

Remember that your real cost of owning a car is your total owning and operating cost:

    Purchase Price
+   Interest and loan costs (if any)
+   Insurance (much higher for some cars than others)
+   Repairs and Maintenance
+   Fuel and other Operating costs
(-) Resale Price (when you eventually sell it)
=   Total Cost

So pick the car that gives you the best balance of value and function, based on the reasons you are buying the car. Keep in mind at all times, you are the best expert as to how to spend your money to get what you want.

Pick The Car That Gives You The
Best <u>Balance</u> Of Value And Function

Shop, Shop, Shop

Now you have a list of what you might want and an idea of the price range you might have to pay. Where will you find the best deal?

Promise yourself you will look at 4 or 5 cars (at least) before you make any decisions. Comparison shopping is the best way to get what's best for you at the lowest possible cost. Leave your checkbook at home at first to reduce the temptation. Many salesmen will push you very hard to close the sale *today,* because that's how they are trained, measured, and paid. But it's not in your best interest to make a hasty decision. There will be lots of good cars available tomorrow, too. Even if that one you think you *really* want is gone tomorrow (unlikely), there will be another one as good or better. So keep shopping.

While you are shopping, be certain to qualify yourself to the seller as a real buyer. Tell them what you intend to do and when. If you would prefer to be left alone to look through the car lot, tell them so. But you will not be able to properly negotiate prices until they believe you are a serious buyer who has the potential to be a customer *now.* The salesman will probably not consider you a serious buyer unless you show a focus on a specific model or two and he believes he can get you to buy something today.

You might also find it helpful to write out your car specs on a slip of paper along with your name and phone number and leave it with the car salesman. Be very specific about what you *require* and what other items might be optional.

There are at least five places you might find the car you will buy: From a friend, another individual, a new-car dealer, a used-car dealer, or an auction.

You may be surprised to learn that almost 25% of the used cars sold in the U.S. were sold between acquaintances! This is about twice as many as all the used-car dealer lots and about the same as were sold between individuals who were not acquaintances. New car dealers sold almost half of the used cars in the U.S.

You should consider all of these sources. Any one of them may turn up the right car for you at a good price. We'll look at each one more closely.

Friends

All of us know of a friend or acquaintance who is selling his car or talking about selling it. It may be an excellent car or it may be a real problem. We probably know which! That is one of the advantages of buying from someone we know. They are the most likely of all sources to tell us the truth about a potential car purchase (but not always). And they will often agree to a very reasonable selling price. If we pay them what a dealer will actually give them on a trade-in basis, we are likely to save one or two thousand dollars compared to the price the dealer will put on the car when he puts it on his used-car lot.

So be sure to let your friends know you are in the market for a car. You could end up with a car you already know about at a very reasonable price.

Individuals

The morning newspaper, the weekly community shopper's newspaper, community bulletin boards, and even the weekend flea market are all sources of cars for sale by individuals. Generally you will find that cars from individuals are priced a little lower than cars from dealers - often somewhere between wholesale and retail prices.

But be a little cautious. Some of these are amateurs like us who are selling their cars for a variety of good reasons. And some of these individuals are professionals who sell cars for a living or at least make money on the side - what is called "curbstoning" cars. These curbstoners may be perfectly legitimate and may offer a really good value, or they may be selling a dolled-up wreck or a real problem car. Often they bought the car at a wholesale auction and don't know much about the background of the car. So they really can't help you with very much meaningful information on which you can make a decision. Ask how long they have owned the car and why they are selling it. A legitimate curbstoner will have no problem telling you about what he is doing. He is really a dealer without a car lot - a professional in the used-car business. Beware if the person is vague or evasive about their activities. You would be smart to move on.

An important part of buying a car from an individual is asking him the right questions. Ask first over the phone and then again in person. Consistent answers are more likely to be the truth! While we are speaking of truth, be aware that you are most likely to find a car mis-represented when you are dealing with an individual. Car dealers have a lot of people looking over their shoulder and there are now some tough laws for those that cheat the public. Plus, an established dealer values his reputation in the community and wants to sell you a good car without problems so that you will return to buy another. And if you are happy with him you will tell your friends.

Consistent Answers Are More Likely To Be The Truth

But an individual is sometimes fairly desperate to sell his car. Whether it is a good car or not, he needs to get rid of it. This is the only sale he ever plans to make to you, so he is probably not worried about reputation or "bending the truth". He is more likely to turn the odometer back or forget to tell you about a major wreck or other major problem with the car. Your questions and a thorough check-out (Chapter 4) are likely to detect these problems.

Notice that many of the questions are not specific or lead-
ing as to what you are after. You are looking for the way
the person answers the question as well as the specific
information. This gives you a feel for the person as well as
the car.

Incidentally, it's best to meet the person at his home
instead of a shopping center or parking lot. This gives you
a chance to look at his other car(s) and his house and yard.
Does he appear to be careful and neat? Or is everything
he owns in disarray and in serious need of maintenance?
It's a safe bet that the car you are looking at has been
treated the same way as everything else you see.

QUESTIONS

1. "What is the car like?" Size up how much the seller
    knows about the car and the equipment on it.
2. "What condition is it in?" Follow with "What will I
    need to do to put it in top condition?" Be sure to
    write down the responses. Any specific mention is
    an area to investigate if/when you see the car.
3. "Who does the maintenance on the car?" Good
    maintenance done on-time makes a better used car.
    A car that has been carelessly maintained has a
    better chance of being a problem for you. Listen
    carefully.
4. "Why are you selling it?" Is it a bad or unreliable
    car they don't want or are they getting a newer or
    bigger or different kind of vehicle?
5. "How long has it been for sale?" The longer it has
    been for sale the more flexible the seller. Or, maybe
    others have seen problems in the car they didn't
    want.

6. "Has the car been in an accident?" If so, get specifics as to when and how much damage to what part of the car.
7. "Where did you get the car and when?" Who owned it before? Did it come from an area of the country that uses a lot of road salt in the winter?
8. "What is the price of the car?" Listening closely to the answer will give you some idea of how firm the price may be. "I'd like to get..." "I think it's worth..." "Book price is..." (*whose* book?!) Don't be quick in responding. A slight pause here will be more uncomfortable for the seller than the buyer and you could get another indication of some price flexibility.
9. Always finish with "What is the least you would accept?" But don't assume that this is actually the absolute lowest price you can expect to get.

New-Car Dealers

The most popular source of used cars is the new-car dealer. They will generally keep the best, cleanest, lowest-mileage trade-ins to put on their own used-car lot. The rough ones with high mileage and problems they generally wholesale to auction companies or other used-car dealers.

So they are likely to have some of the best used cars in town - but not the cheapest. They have above-average cars, probably at above-average prices. They have the service facilities and staff to help you with your car before and after you buy it. If they have been around for a while they probably work hard to build a reputation for quality and service. And you probably know something about their reputation. Pay attention to it.

They are the most likely of all used-car sources to do a reasonable job of helping you with a problem after you buy a used car. Although most are sold on an as-is basis without any warranty, they often will help you with a problem after you buy the car, especially if it happens soon after you buy it or if for some reason the car does not turn out to be as represented by them. Remember, they often don't know everything about the car, either. Their customers trade in cars that have been in accidents or that have major problems that they don't tell the dealer about. And the dealer may or may not find that surprise before you buy the car. It is a *used* car, and you can't expect the dealer to cover all the risks.

Therefore it is important that you do a thorough job of checking out the car before you buy it. You may save yourself - and the dealer - a lot of grief.

One last advantage of new-car dealers is that they are likely to be able to tell you who the former owner was. If you can find out, by all means call. Ask the previous owner the same questions listed above for the individual seller. He might even be more honest with you than he was with the dealer when he traded the car. You will almost certainly get a good idea of whether the former owner liked the car a lot or was happy to get rid of it. Don't hesitate to ask.

There is a special ploy that car dealers sometimes use. It's called "But look what we have in it". When they take a car in trade, they can give the car buyer a nice high retail "trade-in" price for his own car. Then he feels great and can brag to his friends about what a terrific price he got for his old car - "$1000 over book, you guys". Of course he may have paid $1000 more for his new car than he could have gotten with shrewd bargaining. So now the dealer has this good used car and can show the prospective buyer of that car "how much they have in the car". Which may be misleading. But it makes everybody happy. The salesman makes more commission and the dealer makes more on the whole transaction.

But Look What We Have In It...

Or maybe the dealer has actually paid too much for the car. It does happen. But don't be swayed by how much *they* have in the car. What's important to you is - how much is it worth to *you* compared to other cars?

Used-Car Dealers

The used-car dealer is similar to the new-car dealer in some ways but quite different in others. His cars are usually lower priced. He generally has lower overhead than the new-car dealer. He will have a greater variety of makes and models, especially at the lower-price end of the market. And his only business is finding you the used car you want.

He has acquired many of his cars through auction or other dealers and may have no real idea where they came from originally. If he is an established dealer, he may have some cars he knows about, have taken in on trade for newer used cars, or simply know the owner. Be sure to ask. It's always valuable talking to the previous owner.

The used-car dealer does not have the service staff and facility (or the overhead) to help you with car problems after you buy it. He may have a mechanic to help spruce up acquired cars before they are put on the lot, but nothing like the new-car dealer. He may not even have a mechanic at all. He probably relies on his own expertise to sort good cars from bad ones with a quick inspection. And he's probably pretty good at it if he's been there any time at all. His survival depends on these skills - and his ability to negotiate with you. But again, it's in your best interest as well as his to check the car out thoroughly before you decide to buy it.

Auto Rental Agencies

A special kind of used-car dealer is the auto rental agency. They regularly turn over a quantity of used cars

from their rental fleet. They often have reasonable mileage and have been properly maintained. The prices are
reasonable and service records are often available.

Although some of the cars may have had occasional
hard use, they are not driven until they start having problems. They are usually driven by business people and are
maintained better than most cars owned by individuals.
Although they will never be offered as low-mileage cars,
they are usually sold before the mileage is excessive so
that they bring a better price. They will usually not
knowingly sell you a "problem car".

This is a perfectly legitimate source of good used cars.
They may not often advertise in the newspaper auto classified section, but they are listed in the yellow pages and
are probably located near the airport or on a major road
with a lot of other car dealers.

Another category of cars similar to rentals are fleet cars
from major corporations. These may be resold through
the leasing agency or through the new-car dealer and may
offer an excellent buy. You may even be able to find out
the name of the specific person who drove the car. Talking to this person will add significantly to your knowledge
of the condition of the car and its value to you.

Auctions

The most risky place to buy a used car is, without a
doubt, an auction. It may be bank auction, an estate sale,
or it may be a "Dealer-only" auction that a friend has
brought you to. The prices are generally 30% below retail, which sounds very attractive.

But be careful! The auctioneers and most of the customers know what they are doing there. They have done
it many times before. The cars are most often problem
cars from dealers or repossessions from people in financial
trouble. You probably won't get a chance to drive any of
the cars ahead of time or do any serious evaluation of their
condition.

You will be bidding against pros in a very fast-paced
event. Do yourself a favor and don't ever go to your first
auction to buy a car. Go the first time and just watch and
learn. Take an expert with you if you can and you will
learn more. You might even be required to be escorted
by dealer or someone who is a "member" of whatever group
is running the auction.

You will need to take cash or a cashier's check with
you to the auction. You will usually be required to make
a 25% deposit on your purchase and pay the balance within
two days.

If you are a bit of a gambler this may be the place for
you to find a used-car at a bargain price. But remember
it is a gamble. There is a reason the cars sell for such low
prices. Even the experts get stuck occasionally but they
hope to make it up on the average by moving lots of cars.

Pricing

A car is only worth what someone will pay for it. All
the books and guides together can't say what a car is really
worth to you - or how much the seller can get for it. They
are only guides. The price chart below is only an average
of a lot of different transactions. The seller wants to get
as much as he can and you want to pay as little as
possible.

Plain Janes Are Often A Better Buy

There are three areas of pricing you need to think about before you get started. If initial purchase price is of major importance to you, remember these three things:

1. Individuals often price their own car lower than dealers.
2. Plain-jane models will be lower cost transportation than the sporty models.
3. A car that looks rough, rusty, or needs paint may sell for a very low price but be quite reliable transportation. So be certain to separate your ego from your economics. Most of us want a car that looks good, but it will be more expensive and is not necessarily better transportation. For the same level of transportation - year, make, accessories, engine, etc. - the plain brown

4-door sedan with a dent or two will bring significantly less money than the red sporty-looking coupe with the fancy wheels and the removable T-top that every teenager would love to drive to school - even if the original new-car sticker prices were about the same. So if you really want good transportation at a low cost, plain is better. You get the added bonus of probably getting a car that has not been driven as hard as the sporty one.

Look at the price chart below for several different four-year-old cars. Notice the wide variations in resale price compared to original Manufacturer's Suggested Retail Price (MSRP). The data is from the April, 1992, N.A.D.A. Official Used Car Guide. Although this price data is out of date by the time you read this, the principles are not. You can use your own pricing information to build you own current pricing chart and you will find the same results.

Market Price, April 1991

CAR	Original MSRP	Average Retail
1988 Honda Accord 4-Dr DX	$11,175	$7,850
Percent of original price:	100%	70%
1988 Honda Civic 4-Dr DX	$8,795	$5,650
Percent of original price:	100%	64%
1988 Toyota Camry 4-Dr	$10,898	$6,675
Percent of original price:	100%	61%
1988 Plymouth Grand Fury 4-Dr	$12,127	$5,025
Percent of original price:	100%	41%
1988 Ford Crown Vict. 4-Dr	$15,218	$6,700
Percent of original price:	100%	44%

1988 Ford Taurus 4-Dr 6-Cyl	$12,835	$4,550
Percent of original price:	100%	35%
1988 Chevy CaprCls 4-Dr 8-Cyl	$13,115	$7,075
Percent of original price:	100%	54%

From this you can draw several conclusions:

1. A four-year-old car in good condition can be purchased (retail) for as little as 35% of its original sticker price - a real bargain!
2. The Honda Accord and Civic are very desirable used cars - as evidenced by the retail resale price of 64% to 70% of the original MSRP.
3. All the popular Japanese imports depreciated less than the American manufacturers. Bad news when you buy them used, good news when you sell them.
4. Used cars even from the same manufacturer depreciate differently based on their desirability in the market place. There is no fixed pattern about big vs. small. Regional differences may be significant. My son bought an '87 Toyota 4-wheel-drive in Memphis and sold it 28 months later in Denver for about what he paid for it. That model is in much greater demand in Denver because of the snow and it is therefore worth more there. It also showed no deterioration from road salt.
5. Remember that the original "sticker" price is not necessarily what the car sold for new. The American cars were probably bought at a greater discount from the manufacturer's suggested retail price, so the depreciation may not be quite as much as it appears.

Cars sell above and below the guidelines. If you have found the car you really want, it's not wrong to pay above the "high retail" guide price. You are still buying the car well below what it would have cost new. Your time and efforts are worth something, too. When you come across the car that is just exactly what you want, it may well be worth more to you than to someone else. If you can afford it and want *this* car, go ahead.

Sometimes a really good car will sell below "rough wholesale," the price a dealer might pay for a really beat-up car. The seller needs to get rid of it and is willing and able to take the lower price in order to have it sold. So you get a bargain because you were in the right place at the right time.

But be careful. If the deal is "too good to be true" it may be just that. The car may have major problems you have not discovered or it may even be stolen. If you buy

If The Deal Is 'Too Good To Be True'
It May Be Just That

a stolen car, it will not belong to you. You will lose everything you paid for it and even be breaking the law. You do
not want to be in possession of stolen goods! Check the
title and the Vehicle Identification Number (VIN) on the car
carefully. If in doubt, the local police can quickly run a VIN
check with the FBI data base *before* you buy. They will be
happy to help you spot a stolen car. See also Chapter 9
on titles.

BARGAINING

    You can expect almost all sellers to start with an ask-
ing price that is above what they will really sell the car for.
They expect to have to bargain with you. For cars in the
$4000 to $15,000 range, many dealers will have a windshield price about $2000 above the rock-bottom price they
will really accept. Above or below that price range, the
cushion may be about 20% ($6000 on a $30,000 car). If
the car is advertised on TV or the paper, the cushion may
be reduced to $1000 or 10%. What is advertised is the
price they hope to get. You will have to bargain with them
to reduce the price. Remember that the dealer, the salesman, or any seller is going to try to get as high a price as
possible - without losing you as a sale. That's how they
make their money. And many of them are very good at it.

    When you are ready to get down to serious bargain-
ing, consider leaving your spouse and especially your
children at home. Hard bargaining is best done between
two people, the buyer and the seller. Determine who is
the best bargainer, you or your spouse and then go alone.
Children are usually an easy mark for salesmen. They
are less guarded about their comments and may reveal
things you didn't want the salesman to know. They may
end up being more his ally than yours, especially if they

see a car *they* really want you to buy. Also, it always gives you the easy walk-away comment: "Let me talk to my spouse and I'll get back to you."

Your First Offer Is Just A Starting Point

When you are ready to bargain over the price, remember that your first offer will be considered by the seller just like you took his first asking price - a starting point. You will usually end up somewhere in between. Know what you want to pay and set your limit as to where to quit. You can be firm and yet pleasant without being rude or insulting. A smile may actually confuse them! It usually is not in your best interest to verbally assault the other person in any way - or to be too sympathetic. Just continue to push for what you want as a completely reasonable expectation.

You cannot really complete your bargaining until you determine the condition of the car. See Chapter 4 - CHECKING IT OUT. Your strategy should be to check the car and test drive it while being as non-committal as possible. An occasional "Hmmm" (without other comment) when you find a scratch, leak, or problem is considered by some to be a fair negotiating tool. You are not there to put the seller at ease. You are there to look after yourself!

If your inspection and test drive are satisfactory and you believe you may want the car, you can begin preliminary bargaining then. With your check-out list in hand, determine what expense will be required to put the car into the condition you wish it to be if you owned it. Subtract that from what price you consider fair for a car in that condition you wish it to be. What you have left is the price you consider fair for this car. It should not be one figure, but a range. The lowest figure is the price at which you would consider it a real bargain. The upper figure is the price at which you *might* be willing to buy it but you're not certain. This is the range for you to try negotiations. A good strategy is to work to arrive at a mutually agreed-upon price assuming a mechanic's inspection does not turn up any significant unknown problems.

You will expect the seller to move down from his first price, and he will expect you to move up from your first offer. Many will try to "split the difference". One strategy to avoid this is to increase your offer in increasingly smaller increments. The seller will know you are still interested without you having to give in to his offer. A possible scenario:

Asking price: $5,000

                                  Offer: $4,000

Counter Offer: 4,800

                                  Offer: 4,200

Counter Offer: 4,500 ("Fair Split")

                                  New Offer: 4,350

Refusal

                                  Offer: 4,425

Deal

Offering smaller amounts, especially in non-round numbers, gives the seller the impression that you are running out of bargaining room.

It's up to you to use the information on pricing, condition, and other cars to move the seller in your direction. You probably won't get the lowest possible price unless you do at least one U-turn and walk *slowly* away. Make certain the seller knows how to get hold of you if they reconsider your offer.

When you are dealing with a new-car or used-car dealer, be aware that your financing arrangements can affect the price - either up or down. See Chapter 6 on financing.

FINAL PRICE

Get out your list and summarize what needs to be done to the car. If any expressed warranties have been discussed ("Sure, it will meet city emissions limits after a tune-up!") you will need to write them down and have both of you sign it. Preferably in front of a witness. It's been said that verbal agreements are worth the paper they are written on. Recognize that once you drive off in the car, it is pretty much yours - problems and all.

Verbal Agreements Are Worth The Paper They're Written On

Some metropolitan areas require that the seller certify that the car will pass the emissions standards or pay to have the car corrected so that it will - unless the buyer signs a waiver. Read the fine print!

If there are significant things to be done, you could hold money in reserve until proper completion of the task. The best way is to make a small deposit on the car, sign a sales agreement (seller signs also, of course), and not pick the car up until it is just as you want it. This puts the maximum pressure on the seller to do everything he agreed to do for you.

If you are buying from a dealer, make certain at this point that you understand all the fees and extra charges that will be required. In addition to the normal sales tax and license fees, some dealers add additional "service and delivery fees", even on a used car. These fees are usually negotiable. Just make certain your salesman has told you about *all* the charges you will have to pay to drive the car away. Don't agree to a selling price that you thought was the final bottom-line amount and then have several hundred dollars added to it in additional fees. Ask up front about *all* the fees.

If you get close to what you want, don't be so pig-headed as to insist that you won't budge at all. Maybe the difference isn't very much compared to the total price. As we discussed in Chapter 3, if the car is just what you want, be a little flexible. Your time and energies to continue to look for a car are worth something, too. On the other hand, if it just doesn't feel right, move on. It's your money. Make it work for *you.*

One ploy that some people use in the final bargaining is to take cash, especially if you are dealing with an individual. When you make your offer, put the cash down on the table (or fender, if it's not a windy day). You can add to the amount as you see fit. Maybe you will finally have put all the money from one pocket on the pile as your "last offer." There is something captivating about real cash. When you go to pick it back up and put it in your pocket ("Well, OK, but it's a fair offer."), do it slowly. You may, of course, have a *little* more money in another pocket to give you a little last-minute flexibility.

Another way to pay for the car on the spot is with a cashier's check. It's less fun than cash but is safer than carrying a wad of bills in your pocket. Have the cashier's check drawn to *yourself* for either an agreed-upon amount or for your "minimum bid." You can add to it with cash if you want to. If the deal is completed, you can then endorse the cashier's check over to the seller. It's then as good as cash.

If you know the seller or are buying from a dealer, they may take your check. Otherwise you will have to go to the bank together.

Checking It Out

Now you have found a car you are interested in. You can spend a half hour to an hour with it and greatly improve your knowledge of its history, its present condition, and its probable future serviceability. Even if you are buying it from a friend, you will be able to tell *him* some things about his car when you are finished. If it is a dealer or a stranger selling the car, you would be truly foolish to buy the car without a thorough inspection. They will assure you that the car has already been "checked out," especially if it is a dealer, but you can be certain no one has checked it out as thoroughly as you are going to do.

The inspection will be in two parts. The first part you will do yourself or maybe with the help of a friend. If you are happy with what you find, the second part will be inspection and testing by a competent expert who has the equipment to tell you even more about the car and its condition. As we said before, if you still like the car after your initial inspection and drive test, you can begin to negotiate an acceptable price based on the assumption that the car is as it appears to be at this point. If your expert in the second test turns up any significant problems, they can be taken into account in the final price.

A new service in several major cities in the U.S. will come help you check out the car with an expert technician and a diagnostic computer in a mobile van. They can come to the car in the seller's driveway or the dealer's lot and perform a complete test and inspection of everything outlined here including the personal inspection and road test detailed below. Some of these services will also give you the wholesale and retail prices of the car from the *N.A.D.A.* and the National Auto Research *Black Book* appraisal guides. These independent experts can help you check out a car much more thoroughly than a mechanic is set up to do.

Personal Inspection

Always do your check-out in the daylight and never in the rain. There are just too many ways to miss what you are looking for in the dark or in the rain.

There Are Just Too Many WaysTo Miss What You Are Looking For In The Dark Or In The Rain

You don't have to be an expert mechanic to spot a lot of the major problems you want to avoid in a used car. The list below should help you look, smell, and feel in the right places.

1. Overall appearance - Look at the car front, side and rear. Does it look well cared for? Does the paint color and texture match on all the fenders, doors, trunk, and hood? Do the body panels and trim, especially the hood, doors, and trunk line up properly at the edges? If not, the car may have been in an accident or there has been major rust-through on some of the body panels. New paint on an older car is always a warning flag. Make sure it is there to enhance appearance, not to cover up. It could be hiding serious defects that may re-appear shortly.

2. Accident - Ask again. Do all the doors close properly? Is there paint over-spray on the rubber gaskets? Look carefully at the rubber around the windows and around the key-lock trim. Is the paint inside the door jambs, under the hood and fender wells and inside the trunk smooth, even, and the same color and texture? Do you see any file or grinder marks (swirls or parallel scratch marks) under the paint? Are there any missing attachment bolts under the fenders or in the engine compartment?

3. Rust - Are there signs of rust at the fender joints, trim, door bottoms, under the doors (rocker panels) or around the trunk? Look for rusty or crusty engine, suspension, or body bolts - indications the car was driven in an area of the country where salt is used on

the roads in the winter. Major rust is difficult and expensive to repair permanently. But it can also be a cosmetic problem that makes the car less expensive without making the car less reliable. A paint job will not make it go away - just hide it for a short while.

4. Water Leakage - Does the inside of the car or the trunk smell musty? Are the carpets stained or is the metal floor under the carpet or mat rusting? These are sure signs of a water leak that should be fixed. Water can do major damage to body, upholstery, and wiring. It may be simple to fix or it may be very difficult. If it's a convertible, does the top fit right and go up and down without binding? Water stains part way up the door panels may indicate the car has been in high water or a flood. This can cause major engine, transmission, and electrical problems that may not ever be made right.

5. Tires - Do the tires match each other - at least the front pair and the rear pair? Unmatched tires can make the car handling erratic or dangerous in an emergency maneuver. It may also be an indication of suspension or alignment problems. Tires that show cupping of the tread or uneven wear at the inner or outer edges are evidence of an alignment problem. The car may need re-alignment or even replacement of suspension struts or bushings. Look for uneven wear of the front tires especially, since the front suspension usually requires the most maintenance, especially on front-wheel-drive cars. Unevenly worn rear tires have usually been moved from the front. But the problem may not have been fixed.

While you are checking tires, check the spare tire for condition, air pressure, and size. Will it fit the car? If you need it, are the jack and lug wrench there along with jacking instructions you can read?

6. Suspension - Bounce the car up and down at each corner. It should move stiffly and rebound only once after you stop pushing. There should be no squeaks or groans. Shock absorbers are important to safe handling of the car. They often need replacing after 50,000 miles.

7. Odometer - What mileage does it show? An accepted rule of thumb is about 15,000 miles per year. More miles should reduce the price of the car, less miles will increase it. Is the mileage consistent with the overall condition of the car? Look at the brake pedal for the right edge worn off - a sign of high mileage. Look for service stickers on the door jamb, under the hood, or on the air cleaner. Are they consistent with the odometer? Odometer tampering is against the law but some do it anyway. The seller will have to certify the mileage when they sell the car.

8. Under the Hood - Be careful! Don't get near a running engine. The fan, belts, and pulleys can cause serious injury.

    A fresh clean engine may be signs of problems or repairs - or simply a meticulous owner. But a reasonably dirty engine compartment lets you see right away any repairs done in the last year or so. Look for streaks of oil or antifreeze. Check the level of all the fluids. Note especially the color and consistency of the engine oil and the antifreeze. Be *careful* opening the coolant overflow tank. If the engine is hot, don't! There should be no water or sludge in the oil and no oil, rust or crud in the antifreeze.

Look at all the belts and hoses. Belts should not be frayed, cracked, or glazed (roll them over between your fingers to look. Hoses should be firm but not hard or cracked. The hose ends where they are clamped should not be swollen. Check the battery cables for corroded or frayed ends at the battery. This will cause starting problems, especially in cold weather. Remove the top of the air cleaner and check the air filter. A dirty filter will cause excessive fuel consumption and is a sign of poor maintenance.

Check the federal EPA sticker (cars from the late 70's and newer) under the hood to make sure the car is the year it is supposed to be. Also confirm by this sticker that the car is not a California car (lower gas mileage) or a high-altitude car (will probably run lean and poorly). The sticker is usually on the forward underside of the hood but may also be on an inner fender panel. If it is missing, the hood or part of the front of the car has probably been replaced.

Start the engine and look for smoke (including smoke out the exhaust pipe as you start). Blue smoke is usually engine oil, white smoke is water or antifreeze, and black smoke is excessive fuel being burned. The engine should start easily when cold, confirming that the cold-enrichment systems are working properly. Never buy a car until you have had a chance to start the engine *cold.* Smell under the hood as the engine warms up.   Engine oil, transmission fluid, and antifreeze all have their own characteristics odors, especially when hot. A significant leak may be an expensive problem. Look on the ground under the engine and transmission after the car has run a few minutes. Stick your finger in any drips (or, maybe this is what you brought the friend for) and smell. Is it oil, antifreeze, or just air conditioner condensation? You want to know!

Smoke Or Leaks May Be The
Sign Of A Significant Problem

Listen to the engine noises. Is there excessive noise, clatter, or whining? That could be a water pump bearing, alternator pulley, or even a major engine problem. Quiet is good.

With the engine still running, hold a clip board or notebook firmly over the end of the exhaust pipe for about five seconds. This will allow you to hear any exhaust system leaks much more easily. Be *careful* - the pipe is very hot!

9. Inside the Car - Look at the overall condition and cleanliness of the seats and carpets. Worn or torn upholstery is a sign of high mileage, abuse, or lack of care. Try all the seat adjustments and seat belts.

    Check the engine warning lights by turning the key on without starting the engine. Then start the engine and make sure everything goes out that ought to go out.

Try Everything But The Airbag

With the engine still running, press firmly on the brake pedal and hold it for one minute. If it slowly sinks to the floor, there is problem with the brakes that will need immediate service.

Try *everything* but the air bag! Don't forget to try the heater in the summer and the air conditioning in the winter. You want both to work. Make sure the defrost dampers and all the fan speeds work. Try all the windows, lights, wipers, radio, tape player, sun roof, door locks, trunk release and everything else you see.

10. Under the Car - Look again for any drips or leaks. Look at the *back* side of each wheel, the axles and boots, and the drive train. Any dampness or even darkness could indicate a leak which could be the sign of a problem. While you are out there, look in the fuel filler neck to confirm that the "unleaded only" restrictor is still in place. If not, the car has probably been run on leaded fuel (when it was still available), poisoning the catalytic converter - if it's still there - and/or the oxygen sensor in the fuel management system. As little as 10 gallons of leaded fuel is enough to ruin a lead-free emissions-control system.

11. Road Test - If what you find so far is acceptable, it's time to drive the car. Of course you want the owner with you and you want a license plate on the car. It is best if you start off without allowing the engine to warm up entirely. If it drives smoothly, you then know that the choke or cold-enrichment system is working properly and you will not have winter driveability problems.

You should plan on driving the car for 15 minutes or more in a variety of traffic. Listen for noises with the windows up and then down.

The engine should run smoothly and the transmission should shift smoothly and crisply at light throttle as well as under heavy acceleration. Make sure that the transmission does not "hunt" at cruise (45-55 MPH) and seem confused. That could indicate major transmission problems. After checking for cars behind you, feel the brakes at light, moderate and heavy pressure. There should be no swerving, grabbing, shuddering, or locking of any wheel. You should not feel any pulsing in the steering wheel or brake pedal. The steering should track straight at all speeds without wander, pulling, or vibration. The rim of the steering wheel should not have more than about 1/4 inch of free play. Some of the less expensive front-wheel-drive cars will normally exhibit some throttle-steer. That is, under heavy acceleration, the steering may pull slightly to one side or the other. Do a slow U-turn in a safe place and listen for binding or power steering noises.

When stopped, try the emergency brake to see if it will hold. With the brake on, shift from Drive to Reverse and back to Drive. Any loud clunking noises may mean a problem in the drive train. With a manual transmission, the clutch should engage firmly enough to stall the engine with the brake on and the engine at moderate RPM. Drive the car at least 50 yards in reverse. It should be smooth and quiet.

Watch the exhaust for smoke. Even better, have someone else outside the car watch for smoke when you accelerate and decelerate. There should be none.

Professional Inspection

It is increasingly important to have a used car checked out by a competent expert before you buy it. There can be major problems that affect the value and reliability of the car that are only detectable with the proper equipment. The seller may or may not know about them. If the seller won't let you have the car checked out by a professional, don't buy it. You don't need to take the risk.

Since the early Eighties, there are more and more sensors, pollution-control devices and brain-boxes on cars. Todays cars are totally dependent on the on-board computer to decide continuously for every stroke of every piston how much fuel to give each cylinder and when to set off the spark. And some of these fancy brain-boxes may cost over $1000 to replace if there is a problem.

The good news is that there is diagnostic equipment today that can look inside the engine and tell exactly what is going on with all of these systems. An engine analyzer will actually investigate each cylinder for compression, fuel mixture, spark timing and duration, power contribution, and exhaust emissions. It will check all of the high-tech brain-boxes and feedback sensors that make the car run properly. It will also check the battery and charging systems.

Exhaust emissions tell a lot about how well the engine is running. They are especially important if you live in a state or major metropolitan area with clean-air exhaust-emission limits. You may be required to get an emissions test. If the emissions are not within the specified limits, you cannot get a license for the car.

Many of the good repair shops today will run a complete engine, electrical and emissions diagnosis as part of a used-car inspection and testing. You should insist on it.

Without this diagnosis, you will be like a doctor without his
EKG or X-ray. You just won't know for sure because you
haven't checked *inside.*

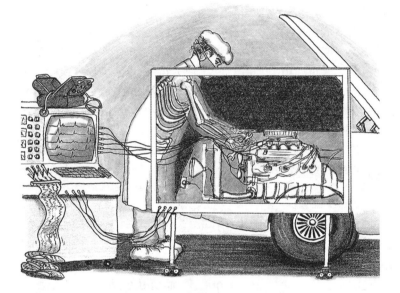

*Diagnostic Equipment Today Can
Look Inside The Engine*

Other items you want checked are obvious - brakes,
suspension, transmission, battery, alternator, and frame.
With the proper equipment, your mechanic can also check
for Freon (air conditioning fluid) leaks. An electronic volt-
meter can determine whether the antifreeze has not been
changed properly at the necessary intervals. Old coolant

can cause major corrosion damage to the engine, heater core, and radiator. This test is especially important on cars with aluminum cylinder heads or engine blocks.

Another important tool is an electronic paint thickness gauge. This is an instrument used to measure the exact thickness of the paint. By making several measurements on the fenders, doors, hood and trunk it is possible to determine whether the car has factory-original paint or whether it has been touched up, repaired, or repainted. This will then conclude whether the car has ever been in an accident or the original finish damaged. Repaint seldom gives the service or appearance of the original factory finish. And major repairs may mean a bent frame or damaged suspension. It's obviously best to know.

When completed, your mechanic should give you a written report detailing what was tested and what the findings were.

Closing The Deal

Now you are ready. You have found the car you want, you know where all the money is coming from (Chapter 6), you have checked out the insurance (Chapter 8), and you are ready to close the deal.

Don't forget to do a final walk-around to make certain the car is in the same condition as when you saw it last. If a few days have elapsed since you checked it thoroughly, make sure that no one has damaged it or removed any accessories.

Ask for the maintenance records and the Owner's Manual (from the manufacturer). If there is no Owner's Manual you should order one from an authorized dealer of that car make. It will be an important source of information on your "new" car.

Title

Before you actually give any money to the seller, especially if it is an individual, ask to see the title. Check the name on the title. Check the Vehicle Identification Number (VIN) printed on the title and compare it with the number on the metal VIN tag on the car, usually inside at the base of the windshield on the driver's side. See if there are any liens against the car recorded on the title. If so, they must be released by the lien-holder before you buy the car. Otherwise they will have first claim on the car and you may have to pay off the lien yourself in order to own the car. If anything looks fishy, don't give the seller any money. You can call the police department with the VIN and they will be glad to run a stolen-vehicle check through the FBI data bank. Buying stolen property may make you an accessory to a crime.

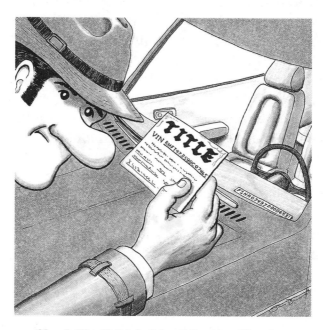

Check The Vehicle Identification Number

Many states require a Notary certification to assign a title. The title will so indicate. For your own protection, a Notarized Bill of Sale is always a good idea in addition to the assigned title. See Chapter 9 for more on the paperwork.

Payment

We have already talked about methods of payment in Chapter 3. You can close the deal by signing over the cashier's check to the seller or by counting out the cash. You may bring a check from your bank or credit union made out to the seller. You may complete the transaction at the bank where you are borrowing the money. The bank has the advantage of having a notary and witnesses present to complete all the paper work.

Whatever the form of payment, it is always a good idea to get a bill of sale from the seller. Get it notarized if at all possible. This is most important, of course, when you have paid cash.

Keys

Before you are finished, be sure to get all the keys (including spare keys) for the ignition, doors, and trunk from the seller. There might even be a special key to unlock the wheel covers, alloy wheels, or lug nuts if the car is so equipped. There also may be a key for the gas filler cap. Some Hondas have a special key to unlock the rear seat to lay it down.

If there is a burglar alarm, be absolutely certain to get the special keys or senders or whatever makes the system work. Insist on getting the manufacturer's instruction manual. It would also be advisable to know who the local installer was in case you have problems. It would be most embarrassing to take your "new" car home only to keep the neighbors awake with its alarm (until the battery died).

Know How To Work The Burglar Alarm

Financing

A major cost of car ownership for many people is the financing. If you can't pay cash, you can borrow the money from someone else, but you will have to pay interest on the amount you borrow over the length of time you borrow it. The more money and the longer the time, the more you will pay. The chart at the end of the chapter shows the total cost of borrowing $1000 for various interest rates for up to six years. Variations in interest rates and fees increase your costs significantly, so shopping for your financing is as important as shopping for the right car. Just like sources for used cars, you never know for sure what will be best for you until you check it out. Just be sure you read everything you will sign. The sales person's description may not be accurate. What's on paper is what you will have to pay.

The basic comparison of rates will be the APR, or Annual Percentage Rate. This is the basic interest cost of using someone else's money over a period of time. It is an out-of-pocket expense that adds nothing to the value of your car and is no longer even tax-deductible (unless the loan is against your house instead of the car).

Be certain you know all of the fees and charges involved. You may pay "origination fees," credit report fees, and any number of additional charges on top of the APR. Be sure you know about them all. You should also determine if there is a pre-payment penalty if you want to pay the loan off early to save interest costs. Before you decide how much for how long, be sure to add up the total amount you will pay with all payments and compare that to the amount you are borrowing. The total may surprise you.

If you do not have an established credit history or you have a poor one, you may be asked to have someone with good credit to co-sign for the loan. That co-signer will then be responsible for repaying the loan if you default. If you are asked to co-sign for someone else, don't do it unless you are willing *and able* to pay off the loan for them. Their financial problems could ruin your own credit. Being a co-signer is serious business. Don't take it lightly.

Think Through Your Possible Sources of Money

Sources

The most common sources of money are car dealers, banks, your employee credit union, and finance or loan companies. Any one of these may be best for you.

The car dealer often would like to make the loan to you when you buy the car because they get income from those loans. They usually get a fee or commission from the finance company actually making you the loan. So he makes additional income when you finance the car through the dealer. If the rates are competitive and your credit history qualifies, this can be an additional bargaining chip you can use with the dealer salesman. And since you are already at the dealership looking at the car, this is often the easiest way to finance, but not necessarily the cheapest.

There are likely one or more banks in town that specialize in car loans. Their rates are competitive and they are set up to handle your loan quickly. It would be a good idea to check them out before you are ready to buy a car to determine rates, costs, and loan application procedure. If you want your credit pre-approved, there may be an up-front fee whether you use them for the loan or not. But pre-approval will speed things up when you find the car you want. And knowing you have an approved loan ready whenever you need it will give you added bargaining confidence when you are ready to negotiate with the seller.

There is also another way to borrow your car purchase money from the bank. Instead of a car loan, you can take a personal loan, sometimes at a lower interest rate if your credit record is good. Or, if you have substantial equity in your home you can take out a loan against that. This has the added advantage of usually being tax-deductible.

If you belong to an employee credit union, this is often a very good place to borrow money for your car purchase. The interest rates are usually slightly lower than other sources. In some ways it's almost like borrowing your own money, so they may have reduced risk of loan default which reduces their costs and yours too. Check ahead of time to find out what the costs and the procedures are for your credit union.

There are many finance or loan companies that specialize in car loans. Some of them will help you even if your credit record is not good, but expect a significantly higher APR. Some dealers even provide their own financing on the less-expensive "transportation" cars. Again, the costs will be higher. And sometimes the cost of the car itself will be higher when the dealer "totes the note." Remember that the dealer has to cover his costs, losses, and make a profit, too, or he won't be there next month. So when he makes a high-risk loan his costs are higher and you pay more.

Down-Payment

Usually you will be expected to put down about 10% or more of the purchase price. Just like a home loan, the APR will sometimes be lower if you put down more money. This is because the lenders have found that greater owner equity reduces the chance you will default on the loan, so it reduces their risk and therefore cost. So check it out.

There may be various schemes by which you can borrow the down-payment. The best advice is *don't.* If you don't have the down-payment, wait until you do. Some sellers may even offer to inflate the purchase price and lie about the down-payment so you can borrow most or all of the purchase price. Do yourself a favor and resist the temptation.

How Long?

The chart below shows the cost of borrowing $1000 for up to six years at interest rates from 9% to 18%. You can estimate your own payments by using these numbers. For instance, if you are going to borrow $10,000 for five years at 12%, multiply by 10: $222.50/month, $3,335 interest paid. If you borrow it for only four years, your payments will go up to $263.40/month but you will only pay $2,640 in interest, a savings of almost $900! And, of course, you will get the car paid off a full year sooner. It is a great feeling to not have car payments, even for a little while.

You will lower your cost of car ownership to finance the least amount possible and pay it off as soon as you can. Maybe when you finish the payments, you can pay yourself that amount every month in special savings account to go toward your next car purchase. You might then get an added bonus of a lower loan interest rate because of your larger down-payment.

So when a salesman (or spouse) tempts you to spend more or to reduce your monthly payments by using a longer-term loan, stop and add up the total extra cost of doing so. It's nice to be able to get the financial help to buy the car you want. But remember, it's not *their* money you are spending, it's *yours.* You will have to pay it all back, and then some.

Loan Interest Can Be A Major Expense

You must also be cautious about some of the "NO PAYMENTS FOR SIXTY DAYS" promotions and other variations on the theme. You will likely be charged interest during that period, even if you are making no payments. So check it out. You don't want your car payments to last longer than your car.

MONTHLY PAYMENTS FOR $1000 BORROWED

9% Interest/Year   12% Interest/Year

Loan Years	Monthly Payment	Total Paid	Interest Paid	Loan Years	Monthly Payment	Total Paid	Interest Paid
1	$87.46	$1,050	$50	1	$88.85	$1,066	$66
2	45.69	1,097	97	2	47.08	1,130	130
3	31.80	1,145	145	3	33.22	1,196	196
4	24.89	1,195	195	4	26.34	1,264	264
5	20.76	1,246	246	5	22.25	1,335	335
6	18.03	1,298	298	6	19.56	1,408	408

15% Interest/Year   18% Interest/Year

Loan Years	Monthly Payment	Total Paid	Interest Paid	Loan Years	Monthly Payment	Total Paid	Interest Paid
1	$90.26	$1,083	$83	1	$91.68	$1,100	$100
2	48.49	1,164	164	2	49.93	1,198	198
3	34.67	1,248	248	3	36.16	1,302	302
4	27.84	1,336	336	4	29.38	1,410	410
5	23.79	1,427	427	5	25.40	1,524	524
6	21.15	1,523	523	6	22.81	1,642	642

Warranties

It used to be that only new cars came with breakdown warranties. Now, however, you can buy a warranty to cover major breakdown on a used car through some major national insurance companies. Policies are offered by many car dealers on the cars they sell.

These policies may be through the manufacturer or through a major national insurance company. An advantage of the policy offered by the manufacturer is that you have the expertise and service reputation of the local dealer to help you. An advantage of the policies offered through an insurance company is that you will be able to have the car repaired at any competent service shop after calling an 800- number for authorization of the repair. This gives you greater convenience and the flexibility to use a shop you may prefer.

Coverage

These extended-service breakdown warranties are not exactly like a new car warranty. In general, they are not an "if anything goes wrong we'll make it right" commitment from the manufacturer. They are more like an insurance policy against major breakdown. They have the distinct advantage that if you have a problem you can take the car to any competent repair shop, telephone the warranty company for authorization of the repair, and get the work done right there. You don't have to return to the dealer.

A breakdown warranty covers breakdowns, not general wear and tear. The basic coverage is for breakage of internally-lubricated engine and drive-train components. This is the big, expensive stuff - pistons, valves, block, crankshaft, transmission and drive axle assembly. It does not cover failure due to poor maintenance, lack of adjustment, or misalignment. All the companies require proof of proper maintenance.

Expanded coverage is available at extra cost for electrical systems, electronics, air conditioning, and engine cooling systems. Coverage is also available for seals and gaskets as well as wear and tear.

Policy coverage can be from three months/3000 miles up to three years/40,000 miles. Other coverage may be tacked onto a remaining manufacturer's warranty to extend coverage up to a total of 84 months/100,000 miles.

Repair costs are reimbursed less a deductible amount, usually $50 to $100. A "Zero-Deductible" option is available on most policies, usually at about the cost of one deductible payment.

Cost

Minimum coverage begins at less than $200 for basic drive train, three months/3000 miles. A complete "wrap" package of deluxe coverage for 84 months/100,000 miles usually costs about $1000, depending on make and model.

All the policy premiums are based on make, model, age and mileage of the car. The larger, more expensive, or sporty cars usually cost more. The premiums usually increase when the mileage is above 25,000 miles and is unavailable above 85,000 miles. Coverage may be limited or subject to surcharge on some exotic imports.

Premium charges will vary from dealer to dealer, depending on their own overhead and how much they choose to mark up the fees.

Do I Need It?

A breakdown warranty is a good idea for some people. Others are willing to do without. They are willing to gamble that they will not have a major problem. It's like life or health insurance. It reduces the worry in your life because

Breakdown Warranties Reduce The Worry

you have someone with you if there is a major problem. For an up-front fee that increases your initial cost of ownership, you are buying peace of mind in the long run.

One additional benefit of a breakdown warranty is that it is transferable if you sell the car before your policy expires. This will enhance the resale value of your car.

What's best for you? You will have to decide. Just like picking a particular car, *you* have to make the choice. Spend your money on what is important to you.

Insurance

Another significant cost of car ownership is insurance. You would be wise to check it out ahead of time. Your age, driving record, and other insurance needs (such as home-owners insurance) will affect the cost and availability of insurance on the car you plan to purchase. The other major factor is the car you pick. An expensive high-performance car may require expensive insurance, especially if you are under 25 years old and/or have a poor driving record. Premiums can run several hundred dollars a *month!*

The most important thing to say about insurance is *DON'T DRIVE WITHOUT IT!* You may decide that you don't want collision coverage (they pay to fix your car if it is damaged), but don't even consider being on the road without liability and medical coverage. The cost of other cars, the cost of medical treatment, and the size of court settlements for personal injury would make you a fool indeed to drive without insurance protection. If you have borrowed money with the car as collateral your lender will require you to carry collision coverage to protect their investment in your car.

A very important feature that is available in most areas of the country is Uninsured Motorist coverage. For a small additional premium, your insurance company will cover your damage if you are struck by a motorist who has no insurance. Be aware that as many as a third of the drivers

Insurance--Don't Drive Without It

in some major cities are driving without any insurance whatsoever. A friend of mine saved $18 a year by not buying Uninsured Motorist protection and it cost him his Corvette, which was totaled by an uninsured driver. His insurance company didn't even cover his very substantial medical bills. As the commercial says "Don't leave home without it."

If you or your family already have an insurance agent, work with him to review your plans and the probable cost of the cars you are considering. If you don't have an insurance agent, get one. Insurance advertising is everywhere. Call a few and find someone you can work with who will get you the coverage you need at a competitive cost.

Many people have had excellent luck with some of the large national insurance companies like Allstate or State Farm who have their own agents and are often the most economical. Others prefer independent agents because they can "fight for you" with a variety of companies to get you the best rates and to solve claims problems. All the good agents, whether company or independent, will work hard for you to get the right coverage or help you if you have a claim or a problem. That's their business.

You can reduce your insurance costs by reducing your coverage. One good way to do this is to increase your "deductible." Deductible is the amount you have to pay first in the event you have an accident and collect from your insurance company - a "claim." Many people carry $100 deductible, but they might save more than that every year by increasing their deductible to $250 or even $500. Ask your agent. You don't plan to have an accident every year, do you? By the way, a good driving record (no accidents or traffic tickets in the last three years) is the best way of all to keep your insurance costs down.

A special kind of coverage is called disability insurance. This will make your car payments for you in the event you are disabled and lose your ability to earn an income. It is another way to take the worry out of being a car owner, but it adds to the total cost of car ownership. This kind of coverage is probably less expensive through your employer insurance program or your own personal life insurance package. Again, ask your agent and compare.

So, line up your insurance ahead of time. Your agent can "bind" your coverage even if you are not sure ahead of time which car you are going to buy. Just be certain to call your agent before you drive the car as the new owner.

Titles, Notary, And Lien Release

The first step you must take after you buy the car is to apply for a title transfer. In most states you must apply for the title transfer and license plate at the same time. All states now require titles for motor vehicles. Some states have exceptions for cars older than the early 1970's, for small trailers, or for off-road and farm vehicles.

Title Transfer

The seller of the car must present to you a valid title. Only the person named on the title can sign it over to you. It is reasonable and proper for you to ask for some identification. You and the seller must sign the title. If the seller is a dealer, there is usually a space on the back for re-assignment of title. But he must be a registered dealer with a dealer number. In most states, every time a car changes hands between individuals, sales tax and transfer fees must be paid. It is improper to "sign a car over to someone" and then try to sell it again without processing a title transfer - unless you are a *registered* dealer.

Another very important part of the title to examine carefully is the portion on the title that records liens against the car. If there is any claim or loan against the car it should be recorded on the front of that title. Until that lien is released by a proper officer of the named institution, you cannot own the car without them having first claim to it under the terms of that lien. The title must be properly filled out to release that lien. You might have to accompany the seller to the bank to get the lien released. It may take your money to release it. You can fill out everything at once.

Until The Lein Is Released, You Don't Own The Car

Both the buyer and seller must sign the title for transfer. These signatures and the lien release may or may not require notarizing. The title itself will tell you what is required, at least at the time that title was issued. Sometimes the rules change from year to year. The seller should give you a bill of sale, which would be good to have notarized, regardless of what your state requires. Be aware that there can be *NO* white-out used on the title or it is immediately void! So look carefully for any alterations, erasures, or white-out.

Odometer Statement

Most states now also require an Odometer Disclosure Statement. If the title itself does not have a place to certify the mileage, you may be required to submit a separate Odometer Disclosure Statement. Most states now require you to have a proper odometer statement signed by both you and the seller in order to transfer the title.

You May Have To Pass Inspection & Emission Testing Before You Can Get License Plates

City Inspection

If you live in a major metropolitan area, you will probably have to pass a city inspection, including exhaust emissions, before you can transfer the title and get the license plate.

Temporary License Plate

If you can't get the paperwork all in order right away, you can probably get a 7-day or 14-day temporary license tag (just like the dealers have) from your local State Highway Patrol office. You will probably have to have a notarized bill of sale to purchase the temporary tag. The cost is only a few dollars. A dealer usually has a supply of these tags. Some states, like Mississippi, do not issue or require temporary tags. But be careful - do not drive the car into an adjoining state that does require a tag of some type.

Getting License Plates

Got all your documents in order? To apply for title transfer and get the license plates, take the signed title, the bill of sale, the odometer statement, and the city inspection report (if needed) to your local licensing authority, often the County Clerk's office. These offices are usually closed on bank holidays. Avoid the first two or three days of the month or you will likely wait in much longer lines. Make sure you have made yourself copies of everything you have signed as well as the documents you are taking. You will be leaving all these with them and you should keep a copy for your records.

Fees

You will have to pay title transfer fees as well as license plate fees. Usually there is also sales tax, which can be considerable. If you have bought the car in one state and are licensing it in another, be sure to have proper documentation of any local sales taxes you paid when you purchased the car. Otherwise you may be required to pay them all over again.

What To Do When You Get It Home

There are several things you can do after you buy the car to increase your satisfaction and reduce the expense and aggravation of car ownership.

You will probably start by washing and cleaning the car thoroughly inside and out. You may want to take it to a "detailing service" who, for $50-$100, will clean it and polish it to look almost like new. Most of us feel a bit of pride when we acquire our "new" car and when it looks good we like our new acquisition even better. Or maybe you enjoy doing this work yourself. Keeping the finish clean and waxed is certainly a good way to help protect your investment.

There are other maintenance items you must keep up with also. Changing oil and filter, lubricating, and servicing the car at regular intervals will mean a substantial difference in the life of your car. Many people do this more often than the manufacturer's recommendations. For instance, the owner's manual may call for an oil change every 7500 miles. But many people will change it at 3000 or 4000 miles, especially if your driving is a lot of start/stop, short-trip city driving. With careful regular maintenance, some car owners have gotten 200,000 miles or more on the same engine. Maintenance makes a big difference and saves money in the long run.

But how do you know what to do and when? You need to start with the owner's manual.

Manuals

The first step is to get the manufacturer's owner's manual if there is not one in the car. You can find out how to order one from the local dealer of that marquee. Their parts department can get one for you.

This owner's manual is an important source of information for your specific car. It tells you where all the accessories are and how they work. It gives you tips on starting and running the car, especially helpful in very cold weather. On some of the newer cars, you are not supposed to even TOUCH the accelerator pedal when starting - the computer does it all. The manual will also tell you how to check all the fluids, when to replace them, and with what. These are things you need to know, and the owner's manual is the best source of that information. When you do get it, sit down and read it cover-to-cover.

Are you going to do some of the maintenance yourself? Perhaps you like the economy of changing your own oil, antifreeze or battery or doing your own tune-ups. If you are even going to pump your own gas and check your own oil on a regular basis, you should also buy an after-market do-it-yourself repair manual. Your favorite car parts place (e.g. Autozone or NAPA) will have one or can get you one. Even if you plan on doing little more than opening the hood occasionally, it will help you recognize simple things you can do yourself versus the more challenging tasks that you should leave to a professional.

An Owner's Manual And Proper Care Are Important

Notebook

Get yourself a small notebook to keep in the glove box. In this you can record expenses and maintenance. This will help you do the proper maintenance on the proper schedule and may also be a help at tax time.

Auto Repair

Find a good repair shop for your car before you need one. Ask people you know that drive the same kind of car where they get their service done. There is no substitute for honest, competent service. It is usually the result of one or more people in a particular establishment that are very good at what they do. Ask around.

There is no foolproof way to find the "perfect" shop. Cars are complicated and no human being will fix everything right every time. But a good shop will get it right most of the time, tell you what is going on, and charge you

Find A Good Repair Shop __Before__ You Need One

reasonable fees for doing so. When it's not right the first time, they will help make it right. Good service is rarely cheap and poor service is never inexpensive. But there are good shops in every city. You can find one by asking and looking. By all means go by and talk with the service manager. His primary job is to be there to help you when you need help. You may find the right place for you at any of the following kinds of service shops.

DEALER

The new-car dealer for the car you bought may have one of the best service shops in town for your car. He is likely to be one of the best equipped in special tools, parts, manufacturer's information and support for your car. He probably has one or more "factory-trained" mechanics. He will often be more expensive than some of the other choices since all this adds to his overhead. The quality of his service depends heavily on the dealership's attitude toward service, the capabilities of the service manager, and skills of the mechanic he has work on your car. Some dealers work very hard to keep your service business after your new-car warranty expires. Check out their reputation with other car owners.

INDEPENDENT

The independent garage is as good as the owner and mechanics. There are excellent independent shops where the owner works with his mechanics every day and makes sure everything is done correctly. Sometimes they specialize in one or two particular brands of cars. Or perhaps "foreign" or "domestic," although that is getting to be a thing of the past as auto manufacturing becomes more and more international. Their overhead and therefore their prices will usually be lower than the car dealer. Again, the best way find a good place is to ask other car owners.

CHAIN STORE

Many stores have an automotive service department. Sears and K-Mart are well-known examples. Others are in the auto service business exclusively, such as Firestone and Goodyear. Their service is often less expensive than the dealer or the independent garage. They run "specials" on brakes, tune-ups, oil changes, and the like which can reduce your costs even further. Some offer excellent warranties on their parts or service. They may be a good source for new tires and suspension work. They work to establish a credible national reputation, which can be a help if you have a problem with their service. They do not usually employ the most experienced mechanics. They will usually not do major overhaul work but can handle most car problems. The service people are often on commission, so be careful when they recommend extra work. Make sure your car really needs it.

SPECIALTY STORE

Tune-up shops, tire and battery shops, muffler shops, and oil-change specialists are good places for specific needs. They may be local or part of a national chain. They are focused in a particular area and may be the lowest-cost way of getting decent service in that special area. Again, watch for specials and week-end discounts. These service people are probably on commission also.

SERVICE STATION

This is just a smaller version of the independent garage. What you get here is highly variable and depends

almost entirely on the person who runs it. Ask around.
Most gas stations are no longer "service stations," but the
older stations may have a lift or two and have someone
who is very good at looking after your car. They may be
right in your neighborhood and therefore very convenient.
Good service is likely to be more personal than at some of
the other service shops. You will probably be on a first-
name basis. This is appealing to some people.

COST OF REPAIRS

Don't hesitate to get more than one estimate on a major
repair. If you know what needs being done, this can often
be done over the phone. If you need to have the shop
examine the car, sometimes there will be a fee for the time
it takes. Get a written estimate, and make sure the shop
understands that they must call you to get your authorization for any additional work. Be sure that the estimate
includes the time that the car will be out of service. Whether
or not the shop can help you with a rental or loaner car in
the meantime may be a factor also. A car dealer is the
most likely to have a loaner car for you, but probably only
for major repairs. And sometimes there will be a rental
charge for the car.

Always ask them to save any parts they remove or
replace so that they can show you the problem. You may
even want to take the parts home with you for someone
else to examine.

Conclusion

Are you finished? Probably not. After reading this book
and buying your "new" car, you are just getting started.

You will buy another one to replace this one, then another and then another. As suggested in the first chapter, writing things down as you go through this process gives you a better chance than most people of avoiding the surprises lurking out there, waiting for all of us.

You have thought through what you wanted, compared your alternatives, shopped carefully, bargained shrewdly, checked the car out thoroughly, gotten all your paperwork in order, and brought home a very nice car that is going to give you good service for your money. It's the American way! But NOW you are a better expert at the whole process and you have your notebook to help you again next time you want to buy a car.

Your notes are going to help you remember where you saw the best cars and who was of most assistance in helping you get what you want. Plus, you will no doubt learn even more about your car as you drive it. Do you wish you had some features or accessories that are not on this car? Are there some things about this car that you would change? Put it all down in your notebook. You may even get so good at this that you can help others buy a better car at less expense. You certainly will be doing a better job for yourself and reducing the auto hassle in your life. But most importantly, you will be able to better enjoy a big expenditure of your hard-earned money. Congratulations!

Appendix

What I Want - Importance of various features & accessories

ITEM   IMPORTANCE

	Critical	Moderate	Some	None
1. Price	X			
2. Appearance:				
Exterior			X	
Interior		X		
3. Condition		X		
4. Reliability	X			
5. Comfort		X		
6. Passenger Space			X	
7. Cargo Space		X		
8. Performance		X		
9. Easy to Drive	X			
10. Safety/Crashworthy	X			
11. Resale Value				X
12. Operating Cost	X			
13. 2-dr/4-dr/Hatchbk				X
14. Sedan/Conv/Van	X			
15. Color		X		
Other Options:				
1. Autom/Man Transm			X	
2. Front/Rear Whl Drive			X	
3. Engine Size/HP			X	
4. Air Conditioning	X			
5. AM/FM/Cassette Radio	X			
6. Power Windows		X		
7. Power Sunroof			X	
8. Power Seat			X	
9. 4-Wheel Drive			X	

What I Want - Importance of various features & accessories (Continued)

ITEM   IMPORTANCE

		Critical	Moderate	Some	None
10.	Seat Style		X		
11.	Cruise Control	X			
12.	Central Locking	X			
13.	Courtesy Lights				
14.	Map Light		X		
15.	Keyless Entry			X	
16.	Delay Wipers			X	
17.	Rear Window Defrost			X	
18.	Rear Window Wiper			X	
19.	Tilt Steering Wheel			X	
20.	Tinted Glass			X	
21.	_____				
22.	_____				
23.	_____				
24.	_____				
25.	_____				

Automobile Rating - Rating of a potential purchase

Car_____ Owner_____ Date_____
ITEM **IMPORTANCE**

	Excellent	Good	Fair	Poor
1. Price	— — — — — — — — —
2. Appearance:				
Exterior	— — — — — — — — —
Interior	— — — — — — — — —
3. Condition	— — — — — — — — —
4. Reliability	— — — — — — — — —
5. Comfort	— — — — — — — — —
6. Passenger Space	— — — — — — — — —
7. Cargo Space	— — — — — — — — —
8. Performance	— — — — — — — — —
9. Easy to Drive	— — — — — — — — —
10. Safety/Crashworthy	— — — — — — — — —
11. Resale Value	— — — — — — — — —
12. Operating Cost	— — — — — — — — —
13. 2-dr/4-dr/Hatchbk	— — — — — — — — —
14. Sedan/Conv/Van	— — — — — — — — —
Other Options:				
1. Autom/Man Transm	— — — — — — — — —
2. Front/Rear Whl Drive	— — — — — — — — —
3. Engine Size/HP	— — — — — — — — —
4. Air Conditioning	— — — — — — — — —
5. AM/FM/Cassette Radio	— — — — — — — — —
6. Power Windows	— — — — — — — — —
7. Power Sunroof	— — — — — — — — —
8. Power Seat	— — — — — — — — —
9. 4-Wheel Drive	— — — — — — — — —
10. Seat Style	— — — — — — — — —
11. Cruise Control	— — — — — — — — —

Automobile - Rating of a potential purchase
(Continued)

ITEM	IMPORTANCE			
	Excellent	**Good**	**Fair**	**Poor**
12. Central Locking	__ __	__ __ __	__ __	__ __
13. Courtesy Lights	__ __	__ __ __	__ __	__ __
14. Map Light	__ __	__ __ __	__ __	__ __
15. Keyless Entry	__ __	__ __ __	__ __	__ __
16. Delay Wipers	__ __	__ __ __	__ __	__ __
17. Rear Window Defrost	__ __	__ __ __	__ __	__ __
18. Rear Window Wiper	__ __	__ __ __	__ __	__ __
19. Tilt Steering Wheel	__ __	__ __ __	__ __	__ __
20. Tinted Glass	__ __	__ __ __	__ __	__ __
21. _____	__ __	__ __ __	__ __	__ __
22. _____	__ __	__ __ __	__ __	__ __
23. _____	__ __	__ __ __	__ __	__ __
24. _____	__ __	__ __ __	__ __	__ __
25. _____	__ __	__ __ __	__ __	__ __
Problems:	__ __	__ __ __	__ __	__ __
Overall (Do I LIKE it?)	__ __	__ __ __	__ __	__ __

Bibliography

Cheap Wheels, by Leslie Sachs, Pocket Books, 1989

Deals on Wheels, by Tana Reiff, Fearon Education, 1981

Used Cars: Finding the Best Buy, by Jim Mateja, Bonus Books, 1988

How to Buy a Used Car, by Joel Makower, Perigree Books, 1952

The Underground Blue Book, by Lee, Diamond S Publishing, 1987

How to Buy and Maintain a Used Car, by Brad Crouch, American Pacific Publishing Co., 1986

The Used Car Believer's Handbook, by Robert Appel, Van Nostrand Reinhold, 1979

Car Buyer's Guide, Government Employee's Insurance Company, 1989

The Quick and Easy Guide to Buying a Used Car, by R. K. Tullos, Commercial Printing Services, Inc., 1991

Successful Car Buying, by Steve Ross, Stackpole Books, 1990

Index

How To Buy A Used Car...Successfully
may be ordered from
Publishers Distribution Service by:

Calling Toll Free
1-800-345-0096

Calling in Michigan & Outside U.S.
1-616-929-0733

Fax Orders
1-616-929-3808

Mail Orders to:
Publishers Distribution Service
121 East Front Street, Suite 203
Traverse City, Michigan 49684

———————————

Visa and MasterCard accepted.
Quantity discounts are available.